What others are saying about *Ready to Love, Fact or Fiction? The Truth about Marriage*:

As a fellow author and treasurer of words, I recognize the power they can have in our lives. Mary has captured and shared her own story with words that will inspire others—whether single, searching, married, happy or not—to reveal all that love can be and is meant to be. With the stories she shares and the exercises she provides, this little book is sure to be a great companion on the journey in search of love.

Angela Wolthuis
Author, *The Woman and the Wall*

The book is a great resource and a framework for people who want to make changes in their lives. It gives steps to follow, questions to answer, and reasons for doing it. It is a springboard to self-discovery and finding the authentic you.

Lorie Shewchuk, Whole Harmonized Healing client

Mary's book provides great insights. I now know that the right one is out there; it's just a matter of time. Thank you again, Mary, for your wonderful book.

Jeanine Smith
Registered Animal Health Technician (RAHT)

I have experienced quite a bit of heartbreak in my life, from breakups to unrequited love. I was always at a loss to explain why I was so unlucky in love. Ready to Love: Fact or Fiction? *has helped me understand that the common denominator in all my failed relationships is me. I now have the tools to understand why I do the things I do in love and change my thinking and behaviour. I am hopeful these changes will lead me to the love I have long been looking for.*

Carli Stevenson
Communications Specialist

Ready To LOVE, Fact or Fiction?

The Truth about Marriage

Jim ~
Wishing you,
a life of Love!

Mary E. Stevenson

Mary E. Stevenson

This book is dedicated to
my husband, Eric Letourneau,
whose love and companionship
inspired me to write it!

Acknowledgements

Thank You, God, for Your support, inspiration, and guidance in all areas of my life.

Thank you and a special acknowledgement to my friends and family who have always given me so much love and support.

Thank you to my mentor, colleague, and friend Anny Slegten for her teaching.

Thank you to Kathleen Mailer, for encouraging me to get my message out into the world; to Jens Petersen, for editing the manuscript; and to everyone at Aurora Publishing who assisted me in putting this book together.

Table of Contents

Foreword

The journey of self-discovery has transformative power for those who choose to walk the path of awareness. In this candid work, Mary Stevenson bravely allows the reader to walk with her, sharing in her challenging relationship experiences in order to learn from her and yet find her own way forward. The combination of her emotional narrative with practical workbook questions allows each person to work out her own solutions in light of Mary's insights. In Mary's refreshingly frank style, she relates her worst days and provides life experiences from some of her clients. Reflecting on these examples, we can see ourselves negotiating the often murky trail from one relationship to the next. Her advice and guidance shed light on how to sidestep the repeated pitfalls and encourage us to courageously walk a new path of authenticity and consciousness.

Not everyone is cut out for the awareness route. Someone once suggested to me that when you opt for a conscious life, it's akin to turning a flashlight on in the darkest, dankest corner of the basement. You might not like what you see, and you can turn off the light, but the image of cobwebs and creepy things can't be erased from your mind. So Mary cheerfully encourages her readers to stand at the doorway to the darkness and flick on the light, knowing that the pain of repeating failures or remaining in a dark situation will outweigh the fear of stepping into the abyss of the unknown—so that ultimately real change can take place.

Susan Smitten, author
Guardian Angels, True Stories of Guidance and Protection

Introduction

Love is something we all seek from the moment we are born. Hopefully from the start, we feel our parents' love. This love is supposed to be unconditional, without limitations. It is always present, no matter what happens; it is boundless and unchanging and non-judgmental. If someone loves us unconditionally, that person may not always like how we are acting, what we are doing or saying, but he/she will always love us.

It is wonderful to have people who love us unconditionally. To have a spouse by our side who loves, respects, honours, supports, and adores us is a gift. When we have someone next to us who helps to bring out the best in us, and we do the same for that person, life is truly sweet! We all flourish when we have this kind of love and support.

From the time we were young, we were given messages about love. I remember distinctly reading fairy tales about the princess who is "saved" by the prince and lives happily ever after. You will see when you read on that I bought into this story, hook, line, and sinker. However, with the man I met—who I thought was my "prince"—I did not have a happily ever after. I will never forget on my wedding day, a fellow church choir member, who was at the celebration, said to me, "Mary, you could fall in love with Frankenstein if he were on a cruise ship. If it doesn't work out, don't worry, just come back home." He had definitely seen that this man was not my "prince." I realized later how much I had believed that my "true love" would appear in front of me one day, as if by magic, and vow to love me forever. Still today when

I watch movies, I see those same messages being sent out to another generation of young girls.

From all the input from different kinds of media—the news, advertisements, talk shows, and a variety of TV shows, from sitcoms to soap operas—it is easy for us to draw unrealistic conclusions and develop false beliefs about how love should be or how we will fall in love.

Despite all the fairy tales though, it is possible to attract a perfect spouse, but we need to be intentional about it and clear about who we are to ensure that the person who comes into our lives will be our "prince" or "princess." Otherwise, we may find that we have someone very different from a true spouse.

In this book, I want to help you decide whether, in fact, you are ready for true love to come into your life. Perhaps first you still need to work on yourself. Exercises at the end of each chapter will allow you to review your life, identify your beliefs, and examine decisions you have made concerning love. Discovering and bringing to light patterns that have developed in your love life will make it possible for you to change and finally attract that special person with the qualities and values you desire in a spouse.

Chapter One

Look at Your Past and Recognize Patterns

The first thing you need to do if you feel you want true love in your life is to look at your past. You may have noticed a pattern in your most recent relationships, but to gain deeper insight, it is important to go back and look at all your love relationships, from the time you were small. Perhaps you developed some erroneous beliefs about love when you were young which you still hold. Perhaps there is someone you always wanted love from but never received it. The most important love in your life, though, is your love for yourself. Can you say you love and appreciate yourself?

At twenty years old, I found that my contented life was about to change drastically in what seemed like overnight. I had been searching for a job in my field (my university degree was in sign language interpreting), but until I found that perfect job, I was working in an office which paid very well and I felt comfortable there. I was also dancing in a professional dance company. Furthermore, I was engaged to a man I had been dating for over two years. My life seemed to be on track and would only get better!

There was an "emergency" in the office; someone had deleted the company's entire database, and all of the information needed to be re-entered into the system for the fiscal year that was ending soon. The company knew that I could type quickly, so I was asked to step up to the plate and help them by re-entering all the data. Because the company had been so good to me, I certainly couldn't say no. I immediately started this big unexpected project and ended up working twelve-hour days, typing for all those hours at one hundred words per minute.

Unfortunately, it wasn't common knowledge at that time that repetitive motion, like long hours of typing, can cause physical harm. The pain I felt in my hands was excruciating, and I was diagnosed after a couple of tests with carpel tunnel syndrome. The doctor said I had to have surgery to cure it. Because of the pain, I couldn't work anymore and also had to leave my dance company. My world was crashing down around me. I was very upset about everything that was happening and became housebound while waiting for the surgery. My fiancé said that I wasn't the same person anymore and cancelled our wedding. (This, of course, was a good thing because I then realized the part of the vows that spoke of "in sickness and in health" was a real challenge for him!) My life was certainly taking a different direction, and I felt lost.

It wasn't a pleasant experience to have the surgery, and I then had to start looking at a career change. I was assessed and told by the insurance company that I could no longer work as a secretary because of the typing. I wouldn't be able to sign for hours either so my career as a sign language interpreter had ended before it had even begun. I was devastated. I went into a depression and started to see a counsellor to help me with these huge changes that had been forced upon me. One thing I decided to do, once I had received my retroactive pay from my compensation claim, was to take myself on a holiday to rest, clear my mind, and hopefully get some insight into what new path I should take in my life.

I started to look at brochures of beautiful resorts, cruises, and foreign lands. I wasn't sure where I should go, but I was looking forward to the trip and hopefully getting some clarity. I was thinking I would bring my brother on the trip, but at the last minute I had a very strong feeling that I needed to go to Martinique to a resort that was very expensive. I couldn't afford to take my brother, but a friend of mine decided she would come with me.

This decision started me on a path that I never could have imagined.

I lived outside the city of Boston and had vowed that I would never leave it because I loved it so much. That all changed in an instant the week I went away on holidays.

The first night at the resort, my friend went ahead of me to get a table for dinner. The club we were at aimed to pair single women with single men. We were placed at a table with two single men and a couple. Right away, one of the men, Bob, focused in on me. He complimented me on my eyes, chatted me up and wouldn't let me alone. We all went dancing at the disco after dinner, and that was it—he had latched onto me, and I was enjoying the attention.

By the end of the week, Bob had asked me to marry him, and I had said yes. This man lived in a different country, and in a city that was thirty-five hundred miles away from Boston. I didn't even think about it. I thought I was in love and had to marry him. (He was my "prince" who had appeared in my life during a time of trouble and woe!) So, I left everything and everyone I knew and moved away. I became a wife, a stepmother, and a Canadian resident all at once, without any preparations.

Because we hadn't really dated, I was in for quite a surprise once we settled into real life in my new home. At the resort, Bob was drinking every day and night, but we all were, as we were on holidays. However, for Bob, this didn't change once he got back to his day-to-day life. I was shocked and upset by this realization.

Life became difficult. I was adjusting to living in a new country, being a stepmother, and being a wife to a man who was constantly changing. I never knew from day to day whether he would be in a good mood or not. I was walking on eggshells in my own home. Quite often, he would blame me for things that weren't going well with him in his work. He would praise me in front of others (and especially his children) and then in private berate me and tell me that I was the cause of his stress and troubles.

I couldn't work because of my immigration status, but I made myself the busiest unemployed person on the planet! Through the church, I visited seniors and taught exercise classes, giving the church the fees. I also created a fundraiser for AIDS research (AIDS Dance for Life). I was doing whatever I could to meet people and try to establish a network for myself and make Canada feel like home.

Living with my husband became harder and harder. I would cry every day from the heartache and the stress. I would go out in the middle of the night, looking for him at bars, and find him stumbling down the street, still dressed for work in his suit. He became verbally abusive, and I became more scared of him and his moods. When I had a big event, like the fundraiser I had created, he would go out the night before and get very drunk and drive home. He knew his drinking and driving upset me. He would sabotage everything that was important to me.

Bob started to spend my savings which I was unaware of until they were all gone. I had put them in a spousal RRSP for retirement. The banks knew Bob from his work and knew that he was married to me so they allowed him to change the investments. He eventually spent everything I had worked hard to save up years before. He ran up credit cards in my name, and we constantly lacked money for food.

I became sick with the stress and started to have trouble eating anything—which worked out well, in one way, because we didn't have the money for food! I became emaciated and depressed. Bob was mentally and verbally abusive for the seven years of our marriage. At the end of it, I not only had a broken heart and little self-confidence, but also empty bank accounts and huge amounts of debt in my name. Needless to say, it was an ugly divorce.

Even with all of that happening to me, I knew I wanted love in my life, so I went right back out into the dating world. I was definitely a "hopeless romantic." Unfortunately, the relationships that followed were not much better than my marriage. Most of the men I developed long-term relationships with were lying, cheating, and also somehow managed to empty my bank accounts. Many of them had addictions of one kind or another. In one of my long-term relationships, I knew I had to end it because his irrational behaviour was starting to have me question my own sanity.

So, I was in my late thirties when I decided that I was a danger to myself and needed to take myself out of the dating world until I could figure out what was going on. I knew I was the common denominator in all of these relationships. I also had learned the hard way that the only person one can change is oneself. I was confused and frustrated with my love life. I knew in my heart that I wanted to have a partner in life, a true companion whom I could count on and trust and who would love me unconditionally—but I always seemed to connect with men who were the exact opposite.

I became a Certified Clinical Hypnotherapist toward the end of my marriage. While studying, I had many personal sessions to release all the anger and hurt that I had accumulated through that relationship. I worked on healing myself and came to a place where I felt more at peace. Hypnotherapy gave me the strength to leave my marriage and start my life over again.

After dating for years and experiencing more heartache, I knew it was time for me to sit in the chair again and start looking at my life more closely. Why was I attracted to men who weren't good for me? Why were they attracted to me? That was when I delved into my past with the intention of figuring out more about me and why, on some level, I was bringing this certain type of man into my life over and over again. I knew something must be going on at a deeper level than I was conscious of.

I started to ask myself questions regarding love and relationships, going back to when I was little. With this focus, patterns I wasn't aware of before started to emerge.

One thing I noticed about myself was that I easily become bored. I like to have a lot of excitement in my life. When I looked at this in terms of my love life, I saw that, if nothing else, it was always exciting. I actually started laughing (you can develop a sense of humour about yourself in this process). Certainly what I had been experiencing wasn't excitement in a pleasant sense: it was in fact something I wanted very much to change as soon as possible, and I underwent a healing on it. I knew, however, that this was only one issue, one layer, of more issues that needed to be looked at.

I know when I first got married, I was in a "down" time in my life and wasn't feeling good about myself. I was confused about what I would do for work, I wasn't dancing anymore, I'd been dumped by my boyfriend, and in general, I was vulnerable. I had lost the "identity" that I had had up till that time. The possibility of happiness and my "prince" coming into my life and "saving" me was very attractive, and I believed what I wanted to believe when I met my husband. All those fairy tales and movies I had watched while growing up had definitely instilled in me the belief that one day that "prince" would come and whisk me away to a life of "happy ever after."

I also noticed that I had always been an extremely sensitive person, with a desire to make people happy. I would often feel other people's pain, sadness, and hurt. When I was in tune with people and could feel their pain, I wanted to take it away and help them. I remember crying a lot when I was a child. Sometimes I didn't even know why I was so incredibly sad.

Being a compassionate child made it difficult for me in school where children can be so mean to each other. Many of the children could see how I cared about others who may have been challenged in some way, and then I became the target. My heart ached also for those children who were mean, for I knew they carried pain inside, or they wouldn't act that way. I wished I knew how to make them feel better too, even though they were being cruel to me.

If I loved someone, the desire to make sure that person was happy was even more intense. When I started to look closely at different relationships in my life, I noticed that most of the men I had been involved with had something negative. If it wasn't addictions, it was depression, insecurity, or all of the above. It was becoming clearer to me that I felt, on some level, that my love for these men would help them to heal. I would try to be the "perfect" girlfriend or wife and do everything to make them happy—then they would be free of their pain and live their lives to their full potential. When I was feeling down, I had an even greater desire to help other people because I felt good knowing I was helping someone else feel better.

Reviewing my life, I knew I had chosen the right profession— being a hypnotherapist and a Reiki Master/Teacher—for I am thrilled to assist people in healing their lives. I find it extremely rewarding to see people's lives shift and change in positive ways. However, I could see clearly that I had to stop bringing people into my personal life and into my heart to heal them. I needed to keep the healing in my office, for when people come for a session, most of the time, it is because they have decided to make a change in their lives, and they are engaged and involved in the process. They must be involved for true healing to take place. I don't do the healing. I assist them in finding their own answers to heal themselves. I understand more deeply now that my role is as a facilitator. Sometimes one has to know that people may make the choice not to heal. It doesn't seem to make sense that people would do that, but it could be that their life path is for them to experience that pain and hurt.

It became clear to me that at the times of these various relationships, I was not feeling happy, complete, and at peace with myself. You must be fully accepting of yourself and love yourself unconditionally in order to bring someone into your life who will do the same. We are always learning, growing, and evolving, but we must know who we are and what makes us happy in order to have someone in our lives who will complement us. We can't have that person "complete" us and give us something that we are searching for to make us happy. We must first find that within ourselves and then share our lives with our partner.

When I reviewed my life and the roles I had taken on in various relationships, I understood how I had created the love life I had had up until that day. I knew at that moment of understanding and healing that I could now change my life to a life that I truly wanted to live!

Often we form our beliefs and make decisions at times when we are emotional and open to impressions. Then we carry these beliefs with us, sometimes for a lifetime, and they affect our behaviour, attitudes, and action without our being aware of it.

At the end of each chapter in this book, you will find a series of questions to answer that will allow you to examine your beliefs about love and explore your own authentic self, who you really are. Your answers will be unique—because you are unique. As you work through the exercises, you will begin to discern patterns and common themes in relation to love in your life, from the time you were a child till the present.

Some answers will come quickly, and you need to trust them. Other answers won't seem to make sense, but write them down—over time they may become clear to you. Some answers may not come at all. Wait, they may just need time to germinate in your mind. You may have answers come to you in dreams, or a thought will pop into your head while you're driving. Keep a little notebook with you at all times so you can jot down your thoughts. Be patient and know that as you read the questions, they are planting seeds in your subconscious.

Notice how your beliefs have affected you at different ages. The important events will come to you as you review your life. You will be able to see how those beliefs have affected decisions you've made, behaviours you've established, or how you see yourself and the world around you. Trust the process and know we have all the answers in us. Take up your pen now and start your own journey of self-exploration.

Chapter One – Love Questions
Date:

When you were young, what expectations did you form about love? Did you feel that love should be like the fairy tales you read or watched in the movies when you were a child? Or did you watch your parents at home and decide that their marriage was what love would be like for you too?

_____

_____

_____

Did you feel love from your parents? Grandparents?

_____

_____

How did you know whether someone loved you? What would they do or say that made you know they cared?

_____

_____

_____

If you didn't feel love from your parents, were there other people in your life whom you felt it from?

_____

_____

Was there someone in your life that you always wanted love from but never received it?

_____

_____

When you review your childhood, what was the most significant relationship in your life? Good or bad?

_____

_____

_____

What were your friendships like? Have you had friendships that were "give and take," or were you the one to give most of the effort and energy?

_____

_____

Have you felt love and acceptance, or have your friendships had conditions?

_____

_____

Look at the person you had your first crush on. Do you remember why you were so infatuated with this person? Was it the person's looks? Personality? Was it because this person was a cheerleader or a football player and in the "popular crowd"?

_____

_____

_____

Or perhaps it was because of how you felt when you were with him/her? What type of personality did this person have?

_____

_____

Was he/she like you or completely different?

_____

_____

Did this person have any distinct personality traits that you remember? (The more you think back on this first love, the easier it will be to remember the details, and the clearer the information will be, no matter how young you were!)

_____

_____

_____

_____

_____

At the time of your first love or your first major crush, how were you feeling about yourself? Were you confident or insecure?

_____

_____

How was your life at home and at school?

_____

_____

How was your social life? Did you have lot of friends?

_____

_____

Were you involved in various activities?

_____

_____

Would you say you were happy?

_____

_____

Did you feel that you loved yourself?

_____

_____

Have you played a certain role with people you've loved (e.g., "the protector" or "the fixer-upper")?

_____

_____

How have you felt about yourself through the years?

_____

_____

Do you have unconditional love and acceptance for yourself?

_____

_____

Do you find that you are yourself when in a relationship, or do you become "someone else"?

_____

_____

Do you allow your relationship to take over your life, or do you share your life with the person you are with?

_____

_____

Chapter Two

Be Honest and Release Old Emotions

If you want to bring a partner into your life who is good for you, you must be honest with yourself. When you look at your past and the roles you have been in, admit to yourself what you see even if you don't like it. There is no use lying to yourself. Being honest will not only help you to attract the right person into your life as a partner and spouse, but it will also heal you in the process. You will feel "freer" in your day-to-day life when you are honest with yourself. Remember that you are only human—and experience all kinds of feelings. It is what we do with them and learn from them that is important.

We all have things in our past we may not be proud of, feelings that we would be embarrassed to admit. When we are truthful with ourselves, we can begin the process of forgiving and changing, if that is what we choose to do. We may even find that we develop a great sense of humour too. We will definitely develop a stronger confidence in ourselves when we decide to change and make ourselves the best we can be.

Looking back over your childhood and young adult life may trigger many emotions. Holding onto old emotions creates energy blocks in our bodies which are not healthy for us physically. These emotions may also be what other people are often tuning into. We need to heal and clear these emotions from our past so we can create the future we want. When we examine old emotions and understand why we felt them, we take away the power they hold. We can learn what we need to learn and release what isn't healthy, be it a behaviour, a thought process, a concept, or a belief.

I had a client, Jake, who had been treated very harshly by his parents, especially his mother. His parents were abusive but felt that placing incredibly high expectations on him would help him strive for the best he could be. They thought if they were tough on him, he would become responsible and dependable.

When he looked back on his life, he realized that he still had a lot of unresolved anger toward his parents and their treatment of him. Peeling back the layers, he also uncovered a deep anger toward himself. He felt that he hadn't reached those expectations and considered himself a failure. This tremendously strong anger was affecting him on many levels.

As Jake reviewed his love relationships, he saw that he had chosen women who were actually like his mother. They were critical and harsh, and he never seemed to be able to satisfy them. Of course, like any child, he wanted love and acceptance from his parents. He chose the same type of woman as a partner to try to work this need for love and acceptance out with her when, in fact, it was the relationship with his mother that still needed to be resolved. Achieving insight into his behaviour started his healing. Unravelling the many layers and issues in his relationship with his mother enabled Jake to look at various aspects of the relationship and how it had affected his behaviour, thoughts, and decisions. Releasing all those old emotions about his mother and their relationship set him free and cleared his mind. This gave him the ability to create a new, happier life in all areas.

Another client came to me because she was unhappy in her marriage. Samantha said that she had everything anyone could want so she didn't understand why she was so miserable. She lived in a magnificent home, had a new car whenever she wanted, and went on several vacations a year. She was a beautiful woman in great health and had three wonderful children. So why wasn't she happy? What was going on?

She started to review her life and patterns emerged. She grew up in a wealthy family, and throughout her childhood, her parents expressed their love by buying her things. This was how she knew they loved her. They were busy with their careers so they didn't have much time to spend with their children. Instead, they bought them everything they wanted. She remembered she enjoyed all of her possessions when she was young, and as she grew older, wanted more. She was embarrassed to admit how focused she was on material things. However, she also felt cheated. When she was honest with herself, she would have loved, more than anything, to have had hugs, kisses, and time with her parents. She discovered that this lack of attention had created a deep sadness in her.

When she looked at her love relationships over the years, she saw that she had always been attracted to men who made a great deal of money. Money was her focus when contemplating a partner. If they spent money on her, that meant they loved and cared about her. They could keep her in the lifestyle she had become accustomed to over the years, but like her parents, they didn't have the time to spend with her, and her sadness continued. She hadn't been happy with any of the men she had dated, and wasn't happy with her husband. She now understood why. She was playing out the same scenario as she had with her parents while growing up. After understanding this connection, she was able to release her old emotions and clearly define what she would like to experience. She changed the cycle for her own children and transformed her marriage as a result.

One woman came to see me because she could never seem to enter into a long-term relationship. Cynthia had dates once in a while, but it never grew into anything more. Although she was a very successful businesswoman, smart, attractive, and very personable, she came for some insight into her own love life.

As she explored her past, she realized that her parents were a great example of a happy marriage. They were soon going to celebrate their fiftieth wedding anniversary. Her parents had always been strong partners, and you could see after all these years how much they still loved and appreciated each other. She was baffled. Why had she never given love a chance?

Reviewing her life and looking at love relationships, she remembered her great uncle and aunt's marriage. Although she didn't see them very often, she remembered being with them a few times. Though very young at the time, she noticed that her uncle did everything he could to please his wife. Her uncle was very different when he was alone with her than when his wife was around. When his wife was near, he didn't have his sense of humour anymore. He was uptight and stressed which showed itself in various ways. One time Cynthia was yelled at by her uncle in a situation which, in fact, did not warrant such a reaction. She was hurt, and emotions ran high. She remembered thinking at that time, even though she was young, that marriage equalled stress and that one's personality changed when one was married. She made a decision that she always wanted to be happy and not change for anyone, so marriage wasn't for her.

Looking back to that time, she realized she had built a wall around herself so no one could get close to her. Fear was what built that wall. She was terrified that she could eventually become like her uncle, giving everything she had to a relationship, even her very self, and never being appreciated. So she never gave anyone the opportunity to know her well enough to form a relationship. She was protecting herself from the pain she had seen her uncle go through.

In protecting herself, she was also denying herself the joy that can come from a healthy relationship. Her perception of marriage was formed at that young age because of the intensity of the emotions she experienced in relation to her uncle and aunt. Their relationship made more of an impact on her than years of watching her parents in a happy marriage.

Once she faced her fear and understood what she had been doing, she was able to open herself up to the possibility of love in her life. She not only was open to a love relationship with a spouse, but she opened herself up to people in general which changed her life in a most wonderful way!

One day, a man walked through my door who seemed possessed of an extraordinary intensity and fierceness. When Jack sat down and explained why he was there, I understood. He was angry and indignant that at forty, he was single with no family. As we discussed his past, he expressed how much he truly hated people. I could feel as we talked how annoyed he was with me.

He had been given up for adoption when he was a baby but had never found a family. Instead, he grew up in group homes. His day-to-day life was chaotic. As he described it, people would make promises and never follow through with them. He was constantly fighting for everything and always disappointed. His resentment toward people increased as he grew older.

Jack realized quickly that his hatred for people was keeping everyone away from him. One could feel the waves of anger emanating from him when one was close. Even if people didn't know what they were sensing, they would be leery of him. He was always expecting the worst from people, and proving himself right over and over again.

As we spoke, he was able to identify the very first time he had felt his anger and gradually was able to make out clear patterns in his life. He understood why he was still single. I felt he had made significant progress that day and had the information he needed to change his life. However, he was still mad at me as he left, and expressed it loudly—we had taken too long in the session. I hoped the best for him.

About a year and a half later, he called me to say that his session with me had changed his life. He was engaged and very happy. He admitted that it had been painful for him on the day of his session to look at his past and acknowledge how he felt and how he had been behaving. He was surprised at the huge shift and change that had taken place once he examined and dealt with past emotions that had been ruling and ruining his life.

Miranda was a client who came to me saying she desperately wanted to have a healthy, happy, steady relationship. She told me that she had been in an abusive marriage for several years. After getting divorced, she started dating again and found that whether the man was a welder, a financial advisor, or a postman, he would also eventually become an abuser. She knew that she either had to stop this cycle or remain single.

When Miranda was growing up, her father was an alcoholic and would physically abuse her mother. Although her father never hit the children, she had been traumatized by years of watching their interactions. As a young child, Miranda determined that she would never have a husband who was like her dad, but later those were the kinds of men she kept attracting.

Her parents were actually still together. As they grew older, the abuse stopped, and it was never talked about. None of the children were allowed to talk about it; it was simply swept under the carpet. Unfortunately, the old pain and hurt was still there, and that energy was attracting men into Miranda's life who were like her father. Once Miranda allowed the emotions and true thoughts about her dad to come out, it was like opening the floodgates. She had never allowed herself to have those feelings before. When she, once and for all, addressed the emotions and trauma from the past, she was able to heal herself.

Many of my clients recognize that they have stored up a great deal of anger, yet they are unwilling to let it go. They feel that letting go of the anger they bear a particular person amounts to not holding that person accountable for the hurt he or she has caused. It's letting that person off the hook. Absolutely not. When you hold onto anger, the only person who is hurt by it is you. Anger is a powerful emotion, but it is not a healthy way to feel your power. Anger is destructive to your physical well-being. When you let it go, you are actually taking your life back and empowering yourself. You are telling that person who hurt you that this is your life, and they can no longer have any control over it. So, please let these emotions out and give yourself a chance to live your life the way you want to.

No matter what comes to light, it takes courage to look at ourselves deeply and admit the feelings that surface. Once we allow this healing process to take place, we can move ahead and take control of our lives. Some people are scared to look at situations or experiences in their past, and that is understandable. However, it is important to take what is positive from those often not-so-positive experiences (and yes, there always is a positive) and discard the rest. Holding onto old emotions keeps us stuck in the past. It also keeps the cycle going as those emotions will continue to bring more of that same type of experience to us until we've resolved the energy blocks. No matter how hard we try to stifle emotions or hide them away, we will still have that energy with us and others will feel it. You will feel the freedom after releasing that energy.

The healing aspect of each client's session is different. As our subconscious mind knows what we need to look at to heal ourselves, it also provides the answer to what we need to do to fully resolve the blockage. Since each one of us comes from a different perspective, the resolutions will be different. There are times when all we need to do is acknowledge where a behaviour or a feeling comes from to resolve it. Other times we may need to establish a dialogue with people in our lives to resolve problems. When we are relaxed, we are able to connect with people on a deeper level and truly converse. This is often when people develop a greater understanding of each other.

Edith was a client who had been abused for many years. She had been regularly beaten until the time she was a young woman. This had never been discussed in her family, and she decided to forget about it. As she grew older, she stopped communicating with her father. During her session with me, the anger she held inside as a result of those beatings erupted most forcefully!

I had her have a conversation with her father while in a state of hypnosis. She expressed to him how those beatings had felt, what she thought of herself because of them, and what conclusions she had come to about men and life as a result. She had never realized how much that experience had affected her whole life. She wanted answers from him . . . why had he done it? She came to see him very differently than she had before—he was a broken soul. Not that this justified his behaviour, but she saw why he had treated his family the way he had—he had been parented in this same way. He actually thought he was doing the best he could at that time. Getting all of these emotions out in the open and releasing them was a relief! Within the next twenty-four hours, her father called her. She heard crying on the other end of the line and was shocked to hear her father's voice. For the first time in his life, he talked about what had happened in their family, and he apologized and asked for forgiveness. They established a relationship as a result of this.

We are all so unique! I have had many clients tell me that through their session, they realized and verbalized things they had never admitted to anyone else before, not even to themselves. It is truly empowering to finally be totally honest with oneself. Sometimes we don't even consciously remember those troubling experiences or thoughts, but once we are in a relaxed state, the memories come back.

Take action now. Go inside yourself and check out what is really going on. We do have the answers inside to all of our questions. The healing process is different for each person, as is our individual experiences. Allow yourself to take this journey, and you will be amazed at how different—and better!—you will feel. When you tap into old experiences and emotions and let them go, once and for all, you are making the decision to live life now, and in the way that will make it great for you.

Chapter Two – Old Emotions Questions
Date:

Do you feel at peace with yourself and the world around you?

_____

_____

Do you find that you have patience or does anger come quickly for you?

_____

_____

Are you aware of what your self-talk is saying to you all day?

_____

_____

Are you kind to yourself or are you a terrible critic?

_____

_____

Write down some of the typical phrases you say to yourself each day.

_____

_____

_____

_____

Do you feel free to express yourself in various situations?

_____

_____

Do you have a sense of freedom in your life?

_____

_____

Do you feel happy as you go through your day-to-day life?

_____

_____

If not, why not?

_____

_____

What bothers you or takes your happiness away?

_____

_____

How do you feel when talking about your childhood?

_____

_____

Are there certain people in your life around whom you do not feel strong?

_____

_____

Who are they, and what are their characteristics?

_____

_____

_____

How do you feel about people in general?

_____

_____

How do you feel about life in general?

_____

_____

How do you feel about your physical body?

_____

_____

Do you have any physical ailments?

_____

_____

Be Honest and Release Old Emotions

Do you feel that you are creating your life, or does it feel as if someone else is in control?

_____

_____

_____

Chapter Three

Find Your Authentic Self

It's been said that we fall in love when we recognize ourselves in another. But how can we find the right partner if we don't know who we truly are ourselves? When we release old emotions and clear out old ideas and beliefs that don't serve us, we are then able to realize our true selves. We are constantly pressured by society, our families, and other influences, but to live our lives fully and joyfully, we need to know who we are and what makes us happy.

We are all unique and different, and that is what makes this world so incredible! Life consists of many different experiences. It is a "black and white" world in that we know what sheer happiness is because we have felt deep sadness, and we know what feeling at peace is because we have felt anger.

We are on a journey of learning and growing, but we are also meant to enjoy life as much as possible! And how do we enjoy life? We need to know who we are, acknowledge our strengths and weaknesses, rejoice and celebrate our abilities and use them to benefit ourselves and others around us.

When you know who you are—what really makes you tick—you can attract the right person. That person will understand, appreciate, and complement you. Your partner certainly doesn't have to have all the same interests or personality traits as you, but he or she does have to be able to support and appreciate yours.

As I look back on my life, I see aspects of my personality, my being—who I am, what I enjoy—that I have suppressed.

For as long as I can remember, I have had a strong faith in God. When I was young, my dad would come into my room to tuck me in and say prayers with me. After he left, I would continue to talk to God and give Him a long list of people I thought needed His assistance. I would also tell Him how I felt about things that had happened at school and what I thought about the world in general! Growing up, I sang in church choirs and felt "tinglies" as I sang to God. As a young woman, I was a deacon at my church and enjoyed volunteer work and visiting seniors. I lived each day in a way that I thought would make God proud of me as He looked down! I started and ended each day with prayer.

Even though my belief in God has been prominent in my life, I didn't clearly see how much my spirituality made me who I am! Reviewing my life, I noticed that all of the men I had been in long-term relationships with weren't spiritual. When I was in those relationships, I still had my beliefs, but I felt I couldn't fully express them. A part of me was put to the side or hidden. These men couldn't appreciate my spirituality because they didn't have spirituality in their lives. Because of these constraints, I wasn't allowing myself to be fully and completely Me.

I also like to have action and excitement around me. (This is probably why I have always had many animals—they always keep me on my toes!)

Through working on myself, another part of me started to come into clearer focus. I have always been a performer, whether on a big stage dancing or at my friend's Gramma's birthday party singing in a corner. I love to entertain! I also like to be entertained; I had to admit this to myself. If I go to a party, eventually I end up telling stories and capturing most of the guests as my audience. I find it exhilarating to be able to tell stories, sing, dance, act and bring joy to others as a result.

I know that this aspect of my personality has caused problems with the men I've had in my life who were insecure. They became jealous and angry with me at times when I was "performing," sometimes on stage and other times just in casual situations. In these relationships, I eventually started to feel bad about my desire to entertain, and I stifled it. I had once again set aside a part of myself.

It was an important step for me to look at these different personality traits of mine and fully embrace them! This is who I am. If I was going to find a true partner in life, I had to first fully acknowledge and love all the parts of myself so I could attract a man who would do the same!

How do you know who you truly are? The first step is clearing out all those old emotions, beliefs, and decisions you made when you were young that are not healthy for you. Then you can start to see your true self. You need to know what your beliefs are, what is important to you, and what you value in life. When you delve into your subconscious and clear out whatever isn't serving you in a positive way, you will find that you had sometimes taken on other people's opinions, fears, desires, and insecurities. You can then figure out how you really feel. When you know your own feelings, thoughts, and understanding of life, you will develop a much stronger self-confidence and become happier.

I have had many clients in my office who don't know what they want in life or what brings them joy. You need to know this so you can have a sense of peace in your life. When you are happy with yourself, you attract the right partner, and then both of you can share and enhance each other's lives.

You need to tune in to yourself. In your day-to-day life, what excites you? Take note when you become more alert and attentive. I describe it as being plugged in. There are things I do that instantly bring a smile to my face. Be honest with yourself. Try new and different things and see what brings you joy! Also, be sure to be honest and acknowledge what you don't like. Be fully aware of how you are feeling in different situations, and learn and explore your personality traits.

I have always loved to help people to feel good and be happy. I once took a course in reflexology. I was fascinated by how rubbing certain points on one's feet helped to heal other parts of the body. I really enjoyed the course immensely until we actually had to work on people's feet. I quickly realized I do not enjoy rubbing strangers' feet. Although I found this healing modality to be beneficial, I knew I could not make this hands-on treatment part of my healing work. I work with clients using energy, and I do touch them, but they are always fully clothed—even their feet! With hypnotherapy, of course, one works on a spiritual level which is comfortable for me as well.

Take time to be in silence, and let your cares melt away. When we tune in and let our minds become quiet, we can receive information from our subconscious minds of what is right and good for us.

It is never good to force oneself to do something one doesn't enjoy. Sometimes there are things in life we have to do that we will not love, but for the most part, we must find what we are good at and what we enjoy, and make this our focus in life. Many times we are focused on making money, but if we do what we love, the money will follow. That is when we are contributing the most to this world. Today, we are so busy in our lives that we never stop. But if you take some quiet time, you will get your own answers clearly. Be aware of your intuition and how it works to keep you on track every day. Once you become aware of it and follow it, the messages will grow stronger. Sometimes we can even get information in dreams.

I have been an avid animal lover since I was a child. I had a relative who was thrown from a horse when she was young and became deadly afraid of them. Without having had much experience of horses, I too developed a fear of them. I had been on some trail rides, and the horses would run me into trees or act up. (I know now that they were tuning in to my nervousness.) I thought horses were beautiful and longed to be able to ride them. When I was an adult, I had dinner one night with friends. The friend I was visiting was a horse trainer. We didn't even talk about her work that night, but when I went home to bed, I dreamt all night about riding a horse. I was galloping and feeling a sense of freedom I had never experienced before. It was utterly thrilling! I woke up and immediately called my friend to ask about lessons for adults. She said she gave classes, so I signed up right then and there.

When I arrived to class, I had no idea whether to ride English or Western, or a clear idea of the difference! I was a little nervous at first, but became more confident with each lesson. At about the fourth class, there were jumps set up in the arena. I was shocked to realize I had signed up for jumping! Panicked at first, I got on my horse and started the exercises. I soon discovered I was enjoying it! During a later class, I did a series of jumps and rode at a canter. I had the same feeling I had experienced in my dream! It was amazing!

This whole experience then led me to using my healing abilities on horses. They are such intuitive animals and feel and respond quickly to one's intention. My dream, and its feelings and message, turned my direction to another path I never knew existed for me. My love for horses has grown tremendously through the years and continues with each horse I am able to work on or ride.

Once you have cleared out some of those old beliefs, you may find that there are things that you were scared of before that now can bring you happiness!

Listen to your intuition and try new things. Allow yourself to explore and ignite that spark within you. There are many forces in our lives pressuring us to be a certain way, but if we know who we are and follow our passions and acknowledge ourselves, everything falls into place! There is a wise saying on this point: God's gift to us is who we are; our gift to God is what we do with it. Know who you are on a spiritual level and celebrate it! That is our purpose on Earth. We are to use our talents, our personalities, and our abilities to the fullest, and thereby grow spiritually and enhance others' lives.

So give yourself the time to explore and discover your authentic self! As you learn more about who you are, you will develop a

Find Your Authentic Self

greater appreciation for yourself. It may take courage and strength to look at parts of yourself that you are not proud of, but this sometimes painful growth will open up your life in many different ways. Be honest with yourself, and your authentic self will emerge. (You know now if there is something you need to change, you have the power and knowledge within to change it.) With this appreciation, a feeling of unconditional love for yourself will grow.

I want to share here an exercise I conduct with clients in which they stand in front of an imagined mirror and describe what they see. Being completely relaxed is important in this exercise, so I would suggest you record the following script and play it back in an appropriate setting.

Sit down in a comfortable place where there are no distractions like phones, etc., and relax. In this most comfortable, safe place, allow all of your cares to fade out of your mind. Stare at a spot on the ceiling directly above your head. As you stare at the spot, your eyes are starting to water and your eyelids are becoming very heavy. As you continue to stare at the spot, your eyelids become so heavy that you must close them, and you relax more deeply. Become aware of your breath. You will notice that when you inhale, your breath is a little cooler than when you exhale. As you focus on your breath, go into your lungs and notice how the rhythm of your breath is slowing down. Any cares or worries are fading away, and you are allowing yourself to relax all the muscles in your body. Just allow the relaxation to flow all over your body. Now become aware of the beautiful light that is in the centre of your chest. Allow that light to shine throughout your body, filling you with your own powerful light energy. It is now extending out all around you brightly. Your energy is completely surrounding you like a ball of white light. This light of yours is protecting you, and as you focus on it, you are tuning into your spirit, the pure essence of you. Know that only your bright loving energy is being sent out into this world and you are open to receive light and loving energy. Only your own light energy is here in your body and aura. We are not what we do or what we have; we are this beautiful light energy. Enjoy the feeling of connecting to yourself on the level of your soul. The relaxation is deepening as you sit in your light and experience who you are in this different way.

As you are experiencing your light, you now find yourself in a beautiful meadow. You see the grass is bright green, and the sky is an amazing blue with just a few fluffy white clouds. You feel the sun shining down on you, and it feels very warm and soothing. You find yourself going deeper into relaxation. Enjoy this wonderful feeling of tranquility as you go deeper down into a peaceful quiet state of being. You smell the scent of wild flowers in the air and feel a slight gentle breeze touch your face. You are feeling very relaxed, and you know that each time you enter this type of deep relaxation, you are healing yourself physically, mentally, emotionally, and spiritually. Everything within you is coming into a perfectly balanced state. Know each time you allow yourself to relax completely, all systems within your body are being regulated, and you are healing your body, healing your life, and healing your soul. Relax and enjoy the experience.

Now in the meadow, you notice there is a large mirror up ahead of you. As you approach the mirror, you know that when you look into it, you will see yourself in all of your beauty and strength, recognizing all of the wonderful things about you. As you approach the mirror, you have a feeling of excitement. You will be able to see all of the incredible qualities you have that perhaps you hadn't recognized in yourself before. As you stand in front of the mirror, you see your light, your soul's energy. Look at yourself and recognize your brilliance. As you stand in front of that mirror, you are becoming more and more aware of all your abilities, talents, beautiful personality traits, and what makes you special in a most wonderful way! Enjoy the experience and drink it in. You are aware of yourself as a spiritual being. You are aware of your connection to the earth below and the heavens above. You are a spiritual being having an experience in a physical body. As you are aware of your light, your spirit, your energy, you are experiencing a most wonderful peace at a deep level. You know that whatever needs to be healed, cleared, and resolved is being done now very easily, gently, in a most wonderful way. You are *more and more aware of your unique abilities, qualities, and what you value most in life. Enjoy this relaxation and seeing yourself in this most special way. Know this is you. Recognizing who you are at this level empowers you in your life. You feel the excitement of knowing who you are in your most pure essence. You are feeling a great appreciation and love for yourself. This love and appreciation is growing now and will continue well into the future. As you become more and more aware of what an amazing person you are, knowing your talents, abilities, qualities, and what is important to you in your life, you feel your power and strength in a peaceful way at a deep level. Seeing yourself in this way, you know whatever you would like to create in your life can come to you easily, gently and in a way that brings much love and joy into your life. Breathe it in . . . See your light energy, feel it, and know it is growing stronger every day.*

You are now slowly coming back to full awareness once again. Easily and gently you are coming back to now . . . One . . . slowly and calmly feel yourself coming back to your comfortable space. Two . . . feel your light energy, feeling great in every way. Three . . . feel calm and relaxed with a clear mind and a peaceful heart. Four . . . your eyes are feeling clear, and Five . . . eyes wide open . . . feeling great . . . full of love and appreciation for yourself.

As you do this exercise, you will start to see more and more of who you really are. When we allow our rational mind to "sleep" and tune in to our subconscious mind, we get the answers we are looking for and can see ourselves so much more clearly. We can develop a love and an appreciation for ourselves that we never had before in our lives.

What we want most from a life partner is to feel unconditional love, but how can we expect unconditional love from someone if we don't feel it for ourselves? We need to know clearly what our morals and values are, what is important to us, and what brings us joy. How can we be happy with someone else if we don't know or don't acknowledge what is important to us? So be honest, be authentic, and when you are, your energy will be vibrating at a different level. This energy will attract a person who is similar to you. Even as life shifts, we will always have those core values guiding us. This needs to be in alignment with our partner. We will shift and change through the years, but if our partner loves, unconditionally, who we are at our core, that love will grow as we do! This is what is needed to keep a marriage together and healthy through a lifetime.

Chapter Three – Authentic Self Questions
Date:

What talents and abilities do you have? Do you enjoy using them?

_____

_____

When looking at yourself, what are your best qualities?

_____

_____

What do you consider to be accomplishments in your life?

_____

_____

What ignites a passion in you? If you don't have any answers, start exploring! Look into classes and see what sparks your interest. Try different things and notice what you enjoy—it may not be that exact thing that you are studying, but it could lead you to your passion.

_____

_____

If you never had to be concerned about money, what would you spend your time doing?

_____

_____

What do you regularly find yourself interested in?

_____

_____

Have you always wanted to try something but have never given yourself permission to or felt really scared to? What is it?

_____

_____

Is there anything that you loved as a child, but since you have grown up haven't let yourself experience?

_____

_____

When doing the visualization exercise, what did you see in you that surprised and amazed you? (Know that the more you do this exercise, the more qualities you will see in yourself!)

_____

_____

_____

Chapter Four

Write Down What's Important

Now that you have a clearer vision of who you are, it is time to write down what is important to you. Your day-to-day life with your spouse will go more smoothly if you have similar values and beliefs. Once again, you need to be honest with yourself about what you really want in your life. This is about living your life fully and freely, so be strong with your statements of what is right and good for you.

When I came to that place of healing where I felt it was safe for me to get into a relationship again, I knew I had to do things differently than in the past. I had clear intentions that I wanted to attract someone who would be my partner for life, my husband. That was one of the first things I needed to admit to myself. Even though I was perfectly capable of taking care of myself as an independent woman, I did want to be married. This time I wanted it to be a happy and healthy marriage.

First I made a list of those qualities I felt were important for my spouse to have. Writing down everything that came to mind, I produced the following list:

- loves me unconditionally
- believes in marriage
- family-oriented
- faithful
- responsible
- trustworthy
- intelligent
- self-confident
- understands and supports me in my work endeavours
- financially stable
- loves animals and children
- takes good care of his body—leads a healthy lifestyle
- physically attractive to me
- patient
- kind and compassionate
- spiritual
- great sense of humour
- likes to dance with me
- cultured and has an appreciation for the Arts
- likes to cook
- enjoys travelling

Notice I did not specify what he should look like or how old he should be. I was focusing on his qualities because as we age, our looks fade, but at the same time our personalities become more prominent. We want to be able to spend each day enjoying and appreciating our partner for his heart and who he is in his soul. We also want to be able to grow spiritually and emotionally with him as the years pass.

Some people will say that there couldn't possibly be someone with all the traits that I would wish for. I used to believe that too. For example, I thought that I would never find a man who would love and appreciate my big animal family as I do—a man who would be fine with having all my dogs sleeping in bed with us. (Some of the men I dated even said that if they were to move in with me, the dogs would have to live outside all the time! Of course, once that was said—the dating stopped!) I decided I couldn't compromise and leave some of the things that are most important to me off my list and out of my life. I knew in my heart that there was a man somewhere who could understand and appreciate my independence, my spirituality, and everything else that was important to me! I decided I would no longer accept anything less than what I knew I needed. So I put everything on that list!

The next important component to bringing this perfect partner to me was to feel what it would be like to have him in my life. I would read my list of qualities and envision myself with him. When seeing our vision, we can only put ourselves in this picture and not that specific perfect partner, but we can envision things associated with having him or her in our lives, like seeing two cars in the driveway or a set of golf clubs in the closet. I would not see any particular person but just know that someone was with me. I would invoke that feeling of what it would be like to experience this kind of love and appreciation from a partner.

I listened to a lot of different music and found a song that would bring on that feeling of having him and being loved. I would read my list once a day and listen to the song once or twice as well and feel how wonderful it is to have this person in my life. I had picked a song that talked about "being kissed from above." I remember listening to those words and feeling that kiss and what it would mean to me, and feel the love behind it. My husband now leaves for work very early every morning, and before he leaves, he always leans over me while I'm sleeping and kisses me. I have that feeling I had when doing my visualizations, and it is wonderful.

It is important when doing visualizations to feel what it is like to have what you are envisioning. Truly feeling your vision helps to set things in motion. The feeling is the power behind the visualization. Feel it intensely, then you must let it go. You have to release this energy and vision into the universe so it can manifest in your life.

I performed this ritual every day for a few months. I was open and ready for the love of my life to come to me, but I wasn't out looking for him. When we are out "looking for love," we can see qualities we wish for in people who really don't have them, or we can miss things that we don't want to see! I knew by following this ritual every day he would come to me eventually.

I made sure I was living my life as my authentic self. I was doing what made me happy, going out with friends, taking dance classes, riding horses, or just taking my dogs out for walks. I knew that if I was honouring who I was by doing what was important to me, that partner whom I was envisioning and feeling would eventually come into my life and be attracted to me.

One night I was out with friends rollerskating and having a blast. They wanted to move on to a bar to listen to a band and dance. I was a little tired, but thought I'd get my second wind once I heard the music. I've always loved live music and taken every opportunity to dance, so I decided to go along to the bar. While dancing, I noticed that a former customer of mine was also on the dance floor. I had seen him briefly a couple of months before at a job site in the city and we had chatted. I had originally met him about a year and a half earlier on a job site out of town. He had bought some tools from me at that time. I remember thinking he was the most polite customer I had ever had.

I thought I'd say hello to him if he looked up from dancing with the woman he was with. He did look up and I waved when I caught his eye. After the dance, he came running over to me and asked me right away what I was doing there. He said he had always assumed I was married with children. I told him that I was single and just out with my friends to hear some live music and dance.

Eric was so enthusiastic about me that it actually made me a little nervous! He kept saying we should go out sometime. I wasn't so sure at that moment that it was a good idea. He said he had known me for so long and still had my business card on his computer. I told him if he did, then he should give me a call sometime, but I didn't give him my number again.

I went home that night and actually dreamt about him. It was the two of us just doing everyday things and living life together. When I awoke, my first thought was that I did need to go out with this man. I went on Facebook, found him, and sent him a message, saying that it was interesting to have run into him the night before. He immediately asked me on a date, and this time I answered yes, and we made plans.

After a few dates, I came to realize that Eric was the embodiment of the qualities I had on my list. The better I got to know him, the more traits I saw that matched the ones I had wanted in a partner. One night during a conversation, he asked me how old I was. It was then that we became aware of the fifteen-year difference in our ages. Despite the age difference, we were very compatible. I was glad I hadn't limited myself to a certain age on my list because I never would have thought someone fifteen years younger than I would be my spouse.

Dating Eric was such a pleasure, and so "easy." I allowed myself to completely be me, and everything flowed smoothly. I had never experienced this before when dating. I had always felt that I should be changing or fixing something so my partner would be happier. In this relationship, I could just enjoy our time together and feel free. I was my authentic self with him, as he was with me.

I told him on our second date that because I practice hypnotherapy, I tend to know intuitively if people are lying to me (of course, it took years for me to fully acknowledge my intuition and what it was telling me). Eric assured me that he would always be honest with me. I was thrilled with his honesty and his integrity. I had reached that point in my life, and self-healing, when I was finally able to be completely honest with myself, and now I had attracted a man who would also be honest with me. It made life so much more pleasant and uncomplicated! One no longer had to guess what was happening; one simply had to ask.

The longer we were together, the more Eric showed his support for every facet of who I was. He has the same philosophy in life as I, so naturally he understands my actions and appreciates who I am. One day Eric of his own accord started to perform Reiki; I was amazed. Although I had performed many Reiki treatments on him, I had not actually attuned him to Reiki as I had with my students in class. It may have come about because somehow I had cleared his energy blocks, perhaps while treating him with Reiki in his sleep. However it happened, it confirmed for me that Eric was without doubt my partner in life. It was shortly after, that Eric proposed marriage, and I joyfully accepted!

Eric's proposal of marriage was fantastic! He knows how much I love to perform and also watch my colleagues perform in shows. Eric loves to perform too. When he lived in Quebec, he performed as an Elvis impersonator. For his proposal, he asked friends of ours if he could sing a song in their show and ask me to marry him. He kept it a secret until the day of the show (although I knew he was lying to me about something—and he knew I knew!).

We had "special" seats in the auditorium. We were watching the show, and as the end of the performance neared, Eric became more antsy in his seat. Just before the last number, he said he had to use the washroom. I told him he should wait; the performance was almost over. He refused, jumped up, and was gone. Our friend then came onto the stage and told the audience that he had always been a big fan of Elvis, and had a friend who was going to sing an Elvis song for everyone. Then Eric walked out on stage! He dedicated the Elvis love song to the love of his life— Mary Stevenson. Wow . . . I loved it! My heart melted as he sang to me—and the hundreds of other people in the audience. Toward the end of the song, a spotlight came on, aimed directly at me in my seat. Our friend walked over to get me, and I then knew what was happening! Eric finished his song, pulled a ring out of his pocket, and asked me to marry him on stage in front of a huge audience! Everyone was screaming and cheering. It was the most perfect way for Eric to propose to me! There were many of our friends and some of my former musical theatre students in the audience which made it so incredibly special.

This proposal was the start of all the thoughtful things that Eric does for me because he is so in tune with who I am, what I love, and what is important to me. At our wedding, Eric had a horse and carriage take us away from the church. He knows how much I love horses, and how special this would be to me on our wedding day.

Eric had never been an animal owner before he met me. Surprisingly enough, as soon as he met my whole gang (three dogs and a cat at the time), he was in love. All of my "kids" took to him quickly. Once we were together for a while, we decided to get a puppy. Our puppy, Sam, was so handsome I thought we should show him. Dog showing is something I had been doing for many years. Eric jumped right in, went to training classes, and was showing Sam and winning! (their first show together). He is now known at the shows as "Shar Pei Guy." He loves showing and often times is correcting me on how to do it (which I find to be ironic!). He now says that he could never again live without a dog or a cat.

Last year Eric was driving home a couple of days before Christmas and saw a dog in the ditch. Two women had pulled over, trying to get the dog to come to them. Eric called to her, and she went to him immediately. He brought her home for the night. When I got home, I could feel that the dog in our dog house was dying. I sent a lot of Reiki to her and prayed for her to heal. We had called around and knew if we brought her to the shelter, she would probably be put to sleep. She ate for us, and we kept treating her with Reiki. Eric said that at least if she died, she would be dying in a nice place enveloped by love. She was drinking and eating more and on Christmas Day, she put her ears up and wagged her tail! Eric said it was our Christmas miracle! I agreed. We looked for any identification on her and put ads out in case her former owners were looking for her. Nothing came of any of it so we decided to adopt her out to a good home as we already had three dogs. We were looking for a family for her and found a friend who wanted to adopt her. On the day we were supposed to bring her to her new home, we took all the dogs for a walk around the neighborhood. I kept getting the message from her that she was at her "forever home." We were her pack, and she needed to stay with us. I started to cry when we got home. Eric

Write Down What's Important

just looked at me and said, "We aren't taking her to a new home, are we?" I said, "No, we can't." Eric actually looked relieved. I knew he loved her a great deal too. I was happy that he had such a big heart when it came to rescuing animals—he has saved quite a few!—and would understand how I and Sera, our new family member, were feeling that day! This is a man who had never owned an animal before meeting me.

Every Christmas since we have been together, we have gotten a photo taken of us to give to family and friends. We have ourselves and all the animals in the photo. This year it was our four dogs and two cats and us. What a challenge to get us all looking at the camera and smiling at the same time!

I signed up for a trade show to display my business, Whole Harmonized Healing. I knew it would be a busy day, and I should have some help at the booth. Eric said he would come and help me. He attended the pre-event meetings, assisted me in choosing what giveaways would be best, helped me to set up my booth, and promoted my business amazingly well! On the day of the event, he talked to hundreds of people, getting them interested in the type of healing work that I do. My heart grew bigger as I watched him promote my business with such passion. Being so fully supported is wonderful. He truly believes in me and the work I do and wants me to be as successful as I can be. He definitely helps me to be stronger and brings out the best in me.

Being married to Eric is a gift in my life. We are so in tune with each other that we read each other's minds throughout the day. Later on in the day, we know we were doing this when we talk to each other! Of course, we don't always agree on everything—if we did, someone would be lying—but we understand and listen to each other. The respect and the caring is immense. I am grateful every day to have a true partner in life. I would love for everyone to have the blessing of this type of relationship in his or her life! (That is why I am telling this story.)

So, start writing your list today (see the exercise at the end of this chapter). Think about what you would enjoy experiencing in your life. This is also a good way to explore and clarify what is of value to you. Sometimes it takes a tragedy for us to do this. You are now in charge. It is no longer an experience in which you are dealing with what comes up; you are now creating it!

Start listening to different kinds of music and see what resonates with you. What stirs up that feeling of being with the most wonderful person who loves you unconditionally? There is a piece of music somewhere that will invoke that feeling in you. Begin to see that vision of you, happy and thriving in your life, and sharing it with someone who appreciates every aspect of you. Feel how incredible life is when you have that person who adores you by your side. See it, feel it, and then let it go, and let it happen.

Chapter Four – What's Important Questions
Date:

What are your values?

_____

_____

_____

What are your beliefs? In regards to

- Religion
- Love Relationships
- Friendships
- Finances
- Work
- Family

_____

_____

_____

_____

_____

_____

Life (How do you look at things? Is the cup half-empty or half-full?)

_____

_____

What do you have fun doing?

_____

_____

What makes you laugh?

_____

_____

What ignites a passion in you or touches your soul?

_____

_____

What do you make time for in your life? (volunteering, spending time in nature, travelling . . .)

_____

_____

What music connects and resonates with you?

_____

_____

Find that piece of music that lets you feel what it is like to have by your side that amazing person who loves you unconditionally.

After answering these questions, make your list. Write down what traits, interests, beliefs, and qualities you feel are important for your spouse to have that will complement you. (Remember, your spouse certainly doesn't have to be the same as you, but you want him/her to understand and respect you and have similar values and beliefs.)

Make sure you are being honest and take time with this exercise. Write down qualities that come to mind as you go through the day.

Chapter Five

Believe and Have Faith

After you have gone through a deep self-evaluation and healing and established your authentic self, it is now time to exercise your faith. Write down what it is you want.

As you read your list every day, listen to the music you have chosen, and feel what it is like to share your life with that amazing person, you will simply know that at some point, your partner will enter your life—when the time is right for both of you. When we believe with our hearts, focus our minds, and feel it is already so, it is done.

Having faith provides a valuable foundation for flourishing! Faith is knowledge attended by a certainty that excludes doubt. Having faith is believing in something we can't see with our naked eye. For some people this is a challenge. Faith-knowledge is not only revealed in our minds, but also sealed upon our hearts. This faith also includes a welcoming of the knowledge. This is when we just know it is so.

It is an incredible gift to have faith in our own power within, and in the power of the universe, or God, or however you refer to the source of all there is.

Today there is much controversy concerning the belief in God. In my experience with clients over the years, I have found that people who have faith in a higher power, no matter what name they put to it—God, Buddha, Goddess, the Universe, the Creator—are happier because they know they are not alone. When they face challenges, they have support, and when they are in pain and burdened, they can bring their sorrows to God, the Source. With God, who lives through us and wants us to be happy, we can also share our wishes and desires.

When we feel connected to a higher power, we feel we are a part of that great energy. We are grounded and content; we have faith in ourselves and feel powerful. It is not a power derived from material things or circumstances, but a true spiritual power from the depths of our soul. It is a confidence in life and in ourselves. When we feel this type of strength and power, we know that we can do or have anything we wish in life. No matter the obstacles, if we have faith that we can achieve something, we will get the answers required to succeed.

There were times in my life where my mind just could not function: I was too tired and worn out to think, so I tuned in to my faith. I knew in my heart and in my gut that my life would take a turn and start improving. When I had faith and let go, the right opportunities and the right people came into my life to make a change for the better in a most surprising way. My faith in those uncertain times remained the only solid rock I could hold onto.

When I was going through my divorce, my ex-husband had run up thousands of dollars of debt in my name. I really didn't know how I was going to pay it off, but I knew that I did not want to go bankrupt.

I had four show dogs and a cat and needed a place where all of us could live comfortably. My parents said they would help me in whatever city or country I chose and to find a place that would accommodate my large family. They knew how much my animals meant to me and how important it was for me to be able to keep them. My dad helped me to find an acreage. Lending me the money, they told me they knew I'd be able to pay them back.

When my dad was leaving to return to the States after getting me settled into my new home in Canada, we started talking again about the money. He told me not to worry but just to focus on being happy starting my new life. He said he had complete faith in me that I would be able to pay him back within two years and also be able to support myself and the family.

If he had that kind of faith in me, I thought, I should have it in myself! I prayed to God even more than usual and gave him my troubles and worries. I had faith that God was helping me to heal my life and make it wonderful. With faith that God was by my side and the faith of my parents in me, I got through this most challenging time and did better than ever.

As it turned out, I paid everything off almost two years to the day that my dad expressed his faith in me! I was also able to support myself and all my "kids."

Faith enhances your life in a way that nothing else can. When you have faith in yourself and in God, you know you can do anything you want in life! Faith is not about the laws of a church body, but about believing in a higher power and that you are a part of it.

So, seek someone out who you know has a strong faith. Sit with that person, as I did with my father when I was young, and pray together. You will feel the power and the strength coming to you. Ask for assistance with a problem or trouble in your life. Give your worries to God, and you will receive the answers you are searching for.

Simply sitting quietly by yourself—becoming aware of your breath and allowing your mind to become calm and peaceful—will let you feel your connection to a higher power. See your energy as it flows through your body and out into your aura. Be aware of how your energy emanates from the soles of your feet and travels to the very core of the earth, how it emanates from the top of your head, connecting to the heavens above. Feel your energy and this higher power. Feel how you are a part of this amazing universe. Know that you are meant to enjoy your experience here. When you are connected to this source, you will be lead down the road you are meant to travel and meet the people who are meant to be in your life.

Chapter Five – Believe and Have Faith Questions
Date:

Were you raised to attend church?

_____

_____

If so, are you still attending?

_____

_____

Do you go to church because of tradition or because of your own beliefs?

_____

_____

If you don't go to church, do you have a belief in God or a higher power?

_____

_____

Do you take time each day to be quiet in your mind?

_____

_____

Do you open yourself up to receive answers and/or information from your higher self/higher power? Do you trust what comes to you?

_____

_____

_____

_____

Do you require "concrete proof" to believe that something exists?

_____

_____

What would this proof need to be for you to have complete faith in yourself and/or a higher power that is assisting you?

_____

_____

If you have faith in a higher power, do you integrate this belief in all areas of your life?

_____

_____

Take time to be quiet and ask for assistance with something you want to achieve. After you ask, let it go. Notice how information may come to your mind spontaneously or people may show up in your life who will help you to reach your goal.

Chapter Six

Go With the Flow

What do we mean when we say "going with the flow"? It means allowing life to unfold as it was meant to. It's trusting our intuition and following what it is telling us. Life flows if we let it! In nature there seems to be an order and system to how things happen. It is fascinating how animals know when it is time to migrate, to mate, or to hibernate. They take the messages from nature and "go with the flow."

So many times we humans try to force things. "Going with the flow" requires patience. If we decide we want something, we can't seem to wait but want it right away! We live in an "instant" society in which we demand things to happen immediately. But quick results don't guarantee quality. When we allow life to flow, things happen at the right time and work out in a most wonderful way! When we try to force something that isn't progressing as we wish, we often find we end up in an unpleasant situation.

One thing that may not feel like "going with the flow" is taking the time to get to know the person we are dating more deeply before sleeping with him or her. Hormones and physical attraction can easily shift the focus of an early relationship to the physical, causing us to temporarily ignore certain personality traits or behaviours in our new partner that we otherwise would have taken note of. The important question of whether we are in fact compatible is often put on the back burner.

If you are looking for a relationship that will last for a lifetime, you need to know who this person is and see if you are in alignment with each other. Sometimes the most exciting physical relationships have nothing else to offer but that. It isn't easy to acknowledge this once you have moved in together or even made a commitment of marriage. So, focus on allowing a true friendship to evolve. Of course, you do want the physical attraction to be there when the time comes to be intimate. If the relationship and connection is there, the physical side of the relationship will be that much more exciting!

I had a client who desperately wanted to have a love relationship and be married. She started dating a man and was enjoying the relationship very much. She could feel mixed messages coming from him but didn't listen to them. She completely ignored her intuition. She asked him to go away on a holiday with her. He had many excuses for not being able to go, and she eventually went alone.

They were seeing each other regularly, but he didn't want her to meet his parents or for them to even know he was dating her. Still she did not follow her intuition and pushed on with the relationship. She wanted to have this man in her life and envisioned a "fairy-tale" life with him.

For his birthday, she got him an expensive gift. To her, this expensive gift symbolized how much he meant to her. He accepted the gift, but still wouldn't give her more of a commitment or even bring her into his circle of friends and family. She started to push harder for this to happen. It was at this point that he finally told her that he didn't really have feelings for her. He enjoyed their intimate time together and enjoyed her company but could never love her or get serious. She was mortified. Looking back at the situation after the relationship ended, she realized she had been pushing things and not "going with the flow." She had not listened to her intuition or allowed things to unfold in a natural way.

Of course, when I started to date Eric, I wondered whether he was the man whom I had been visioning in my self-hypnosis sessions. I had to just allow the relationship to develop on its own. I couldn't put expectations on him or our relationship. I found that this wasn't easy for me because I felt so excited! What I told myself was to just enjoy every moment of our time together and leave it at that. I needed to stay in the "now."

I had to be sure that I was falling in love with this man, that the qualities I was seeing in him were real. Sometimes we can fall in love with the idea of a person, but it isn't the actual person we are with. This is why we need to take time and let the friendship grow at the pace that is right for both of us.

Some people say you shouldn't waste your time if he or she is not the "right" one. But you need to allow the relationship or friendship to evolve, and this can take time. You may not have signs right away that this is the person for you—or not. Fireworks may go off, but perhaps not until later. Every relationship differs.

While dating, I gradually learned more about Eric and saw the qualities in him I was looking for in a partner. When I was with him, my life seemed to "flow." There was nothing I felt that I had to change or force—it felt so "easy" to be with him. I was enjoying this relationship more than any I had ever had before.

In any relationship, of course, there will be differences of opinion, and you will need to learn how to communicate effectively with each other. This can take some work, but the bottom line is to be honest and true to yourself and express how you feel. When you are with the right partner, he or she will respect and honour you and listen and learn with you.

After being together with Eric, I finally understood what my father meant when he said that life is enhanced when shared with a true partner. When the relationship is the right one for you, you grow and flourish in it—which is very different from having to change and accommodate.

In my past relationships, I always felt that there were things that needed to change in my partners or that I needed to change to accommodate them. This certainly wasn't letting life "flow."

What a difference when you commit to being your authentic self and allowing your partner to be who he or she truly is.

So, when someone appears in your life and you start dating, be aware of how you feel when you are with that person. Now do the exercise below.

Chapter Six – Go with the Flow Questions
Date:

You have just started dating someone . . .

Are you relaxed with this person (notwithstanding the excitement of spending time with him/her)?

_____

_____

Do you feel comfortable talking about what is important to you?

_____

_____

Do you share your values and beliefs openly?

_____

_____

Do you allow this person to see all sides of you?

_____

_____

Are you still doing the things that you enjoy doing (hobbies, activities, etc.)?

_____

_____

Are you still living your life in a way that makes you happy and then sharing it with this person?

_____

_____

Are you able to bring your friends and family together with this person and feel good about it?

_____

_____

Do you feel good about yourself when you are with this person?

_____

_____

Identify what it is about this person that makes you love him or her.

Chapter Seven

Make the Commitment

What does it mean to commit? It is a pledge, a promise, an obligation. Making a commitment is engaging oneself completely. It is being there even when it is not easy. It is a trust.

Many people do not take their commitments seriously; they don't understand what it really means to commit to someone.

I see this often when people bring animals into their lives. I live in the country and unfortunately have witnessed many dogs being abandoned on the range roads. When you adopt an animal, you are making a commitment to it, and it should be for life. Many people keep animals until they misbehave, get sick, or sadly, until they become old and need special care. If you are making a commitment, understand what that means and be aware of what your obligations are and be prepared to fulfill them. I couldn't imagine dropping off my old dog on a country road to live out its life in almost certain misery, however long that may be.

Look at the friendships you have. You have friends with you when times are good, you are on the upswing in your life, and they want to be a part of it. Some of those same friends, though, seem to disappear when times get tough.

When you bring a partner or spouse into your life, you need to know that person will be with you no matter what is happening in your life, supporting and loving you unconditionally. And you must give back that same level of commitment. Making a marriage commitment is saying you believe in your partner and the two of you as a couple, and typically you work a lot harder at resolving issues and are not as quick to just say "this is hard" and walk away. In a fully committed relationship, there is no questioning of whether the other person will be around in good times or bad. When you listen to the typical marriage vows, it is comforting to know that someone is saying he or she will be with the other person "for better, for worse, for richer, for poorer, in sickness and in health, until death do us part." They are pledging themselves to the other person completely.

When I developed carpel tunnel syndrome in my hands, I had to leave my job and go on disability. At that time, as I've mentioned, I was engaged to a man I had been with for a couple of years. As soon as I wasn't feeling well and was not able to go out as I used to, he stopped calling. He didn't show up at the time of my surgery and broke up with me immediately afterwards (on the phone!). He was in the relationship for the good times only, and not committed to me (no "in sickness and in health") as I had thought he was. I was very shocked and disappointed, but also relieved that I had found that out before I married him.

At the same time my fiancé was breaking up with me, I stopped hearing from my "many" friends. I thought I had a huge number of friends, from work, dance, and school, but no one was calling (or calling me back). I was no longer at the office or in the dance studio, so "out of sight, out of mind." I had only one friend who would call and take me out for supper and have a visit. He was a colleague from work with a quirky sense of humour that only I seemed to understand. He was committed to our friendship and keeping it alive and well. I was grateful for that, but couldn't believe that no one else would stay in touch once I was out of all of my normal circles.

I was always extremely committed to my friendships and relationships and thought my friends felt the same way about me. They could always count on me to be there when they needed me—in good times and bad—when I was their friend. Of course, if I committed to being someone's girlfriend, I would be there no matter what was happening. I thought it was reciprocal, but I was greatly mistaken.

The question of commitment goes back to the notion of unconditional love. If someone truly loves us unconditionally, that person will be there through all of our triumphs and our tribulations. He or she will want to make this commitment to us and honour it.

Though I was let down by my fiancé and then again later by my husband who ended up not honouring his commitment to me, I still believed in commitment.

Many people who live together for years but never get married say that they don't need "that piece of paper." What does a piece of paper change? It is the action of speaking those words, professing to the world and to God that you are committing yourself to this person. It is pledging that you will love him or her even when it isn't easy to do so.

How comforting to know that someone loves you so much that he or she will be there no matter what you go through. We all want to have lives that are happy and go smoothly, but we also know that life can throw us some curve balls, maybe even some tremendous challenges at times.

When in a relationship, ask yourself whether you can make the commitment to be there for that person through all of life's experiences. Do you love, appreciate, and respect that person enough to make such a commitment? Think about this: if that person were somehow to lose a leg, his looks, or all of his money, would you still be there by his side? Be honest with yourself. If you expect that person to be committed to you, you must reciprocate.

If you do want to be married, say it. Some people hold back on how they really feel. They think it is better to be casual about it, but if marriage is something you want, you need to say so. The same would apply if you felt you couldn't be committed to someone; you must admit that as well and let the person make his own decision on whether or not to stay in the relationship (see my previous discussion on being authentic and writing down everything that is important to you).

So, this finally brings us back to the title of my book—Ready to Love: Fact or Fiction?

Are you ready to love?

The divorce rate in North America is currently about 40 percent. That is shockingly high. Perhaps what we need is to look more closely at what marriage entails and whether we are in fact ready for it—before the wedding takes place. Go through the questions below and see how you feel about the level of commitment required in marriage.

Chapter Seven – Make the Commitment Questions
Date:

Have you considered the level of commitment marriage demands? Is your definition of marriage the same as your partner's?

Are you ready to love and to make a lifelong commitment to someone?

Do you feel that you love and know yourself well enough to know what is right for you?

Does it feel good to make a commitment? (If you feel scared, what is it you feel scared about? For example, do you have reservations about yourself or your partner?)

Look at your partner. Have you brought the right person to you who will be with you for a lifetime? Are you compatible and accepting of each other?

Are you ready to stay with your spouse through both good and challenging times (for example, health challenges, financial issues, etc.)?

_____

_____

How do you face challenges/issues together?

_____

_____

Do you unconditionally love your partner/spouse? Are there things that you want to change in your partner? (Remember that personality traits usually grow stronger over time.)

_____

_____

What is your partner's lifestyle? Are you comfortable living that lifestyle?

_____

_____

Do you share the same values and beliefs as your partner?

_____

_____

_____

Do you both have the same level of commitment to each other?

_____

_____

_____

Conclusion

I hope in reading this book you have been inspired and motivated to find the perfect spouse for you. Despite whatever failed relationships you may have had in the past, remember that your life is your journey, and you can create anything you want to experience—including a fulfilling love life!

For a relationship or marriage to last a lifetime, it needs to be healthy, based on mutual appreciation, respect, and unconditional love for yourself and your spouse.

The journey starts with discovering yourself, but take the time needed for this self-exploration. To know who you are—and love and appreciate everything that makes you uniquely you—will enrich many areas of your life! Explore what is important to you and ignites your passions. Go through the exercises/questions in the book to see if there are some patterns or old issues that you could heal to improve your life—that would allow you to attract the right partner to you. Find that perfect piece of music that invokes that happy, contented feeling of having your life partner beside you.

In the end, you will find yourself empowered and attracting the spouse of your dreams.

About the Author

Mary E. Stevenson has always been enthusiastic about life and a "hopeless romantic." She was born in New Jersey and grew up in various towns on the east coast of the United States. As a young woman, Mary followed her heart and moved to Canada; she has lived in the Great White North ever since.

Mary is a Certified Clinical Hypnotherapist and a Reiki Master/Teacher who has been practicing her healing arts for seventeen years.

She lives on an acreage with her husband outside Edmonton, along with her four dogs and two cats.